UNCLE MIKE'S GUIDE TO

THE REAL
OREGON COAST

Second Edition

Michael Burgess   **Saddle Mountain Press**   **Steve McLeod**

UNCLE MIKE'S GUIDE TO
THE REAL
OREGON COAST

Michael Burgess

with disturbing illustrations by
Steve McLeod

Saddle Mountain Press
Box 1056
Cannon Beach, Oregon 97110

Cover Design by Anderson McConaughy Design

First Edition printed March 1997, Left Coast Group

Saddle Mountain Press
Box 1056
Cannon Beach, Oregon 97110

ISBN 0-9657638-1-1

This book is dedicated to my father and mother, Jay and Wanda Burgess, and to my son, Jason. And to Vivian who was my guide.

INTRODUCTION

There are many pretty guides to the Oregon Coast. This isn't one of them. The author is a native Oregonian who assumes you want the truth. An overly zealous travel industry, and the shameless lies of tourists too proud to admit their mistakes, have created a myth of the Oregon Coast as a holiday destination for the normal to silly, if not dangerous, proportions.

The author refuses to be part of this. He has no axes to grind, no rain gear or sedatives to sell. He doesn't care if you visit the Oregon Coast or not. He only wants the pain and sadness to end. His heart goes out to the gullible who flock here each year expecting things they'll never find: warmth, sunlight, some token shred of civilization. He sees them as victims of a cruel joke. It's one thing to live in a fool's paradise, another to travel great distances getting to it.

Contents

Glossary of Useful Phrases

Acknowledgments

The author and publisher wish to thank the many people whose energies and moral support literally hand carried this book into print. Special gratitude is owed to the Manzanita Creative Arts Council who laundered all funds and supplied a much needed appearance of legitimacy. And to Karen Brown, Our Lady of Microsoft, who looked at our antique computers, laughed, and gave us two that worked. The rest of our gratitude goes to the citizens of Cannon Beach who, in response to our whining, begging, and thinly veiled threats, created a flurry of fund raising activities. Their faith, and willingness to buy copies of a book they'd never seen, is testimony not just to the goodness of their hearts but to their spirit of silly adventure. A final nod of thanks to the bartenders at Bill's Tavern who, through good times and bad, continued to pour beer.

CHAPTER ONE

GEOGRAPHY AND CLIMATE

The Unpleasantness Begins

The upper left edge of North America is a marine subtropical rainforest. The wise vacationer will take a moment to consider this.

That the climate is "marine" implies that it's wet, a clue reinforced by the term "rainforest". The designation "subtropical" means the region lacks anything resembling warmth. "Temperate" is a term often applied, many would argue too loosely.

Other holiday destinations have a climate; the Oregon Coast has weather. The weather occurs in fifteen minute increments so that, on a good (or temperate) day, you may experience several seasons. For those with a ready laugh, a stout immune system, and a love for violent change, few adventures hold a candle to a weekend on the beaches of Oregon.

There are two distinct seasons: the rainy and the wet. The best time to visit is high summer: a break between storm fronts that occurs once or twice a decade and can last as long as a week. Villagers use these freak periods of sunlight to dry their bedding and replenish stocks of bark and fungus.

As any travel agent with the conscience of a puff adder would tell you, off season on the Oregon Coast is something to run from, not make reservations for. In the fall, winter, and spring, precipitation reaches biblical pro portions. The rainy season (all months that aren't August) is a time of funereal gloom and downpour, punctuated by savage storms whose winds tear roofs from sheet metal buildings and hurl Winnebagos into the sea. If you make the mistake of being here, your only thought will be of escape. Flooding and mud slides will make this out of the question.

CHAPTER TWO

NATIVE CULTURE

Before embarking on holiday to strange lands, the prudent traveler takes time to learn something of the native culture. For those coming to the Oregon Coast, accurate information, if not stern warning, is vital. No expedition to the rainforests of New Guinea or Brazil offers a more sobering look at the effects of isolation, despair, and reckless inbreeding on human society. Matters are only made worse when the humans in question were borderline to begin with. The truth cries out for historical perspective.

Historical Perspective

Unless one counts the Native Americans, who inhabited the region for 12,000 years and built what is generally recognized as the richest indigenous culture on the continent, the Oregon Coast was discovered in 1805 by Lewis & Clark, Sacajawea, and thirty federal contract employees who, by the time they'd reached the shores of the Western Sea, devoutly wished they'd never left St. Louis.

Popular history tells us their epic trek ended at Astoria, an especially miserable and storm -wracked spot where the mighty Columbia, or River of the West, flows into a badly misnamed Pacific Ocean. While not an outright lie, this version of events falls many leagues short of the truth. On January 8th, 1806, Lewis & Clark led a small and reluctant group of civil service explorers on a forty mile slog south through the sleet, dank undergrowth, and muck to the present site of Cannon Beach.

(Note: It was actually Sacajawea who led the expedition from the beginning, but she, being both an Indian and a woman, is of little historical significance.)

To say our intrepid explorers were looking for new horizons is to paint an idiot grin on grim conditions.

Forced to winter on the Oregon Coast (there are few other reasons), the ambassadors of western civilization were starving to death and came south following rumors a whale had washed ashore. As luck would have it, one had. Local villagers were just boiling up the last of it when the sorry little band staggered in.

Contrary to accepted fable, they weren't mistaken for gods. The coastal tribes had been trading with seafaring white men (who they thought smelled bad) for many years and were, at the historic moment Lewis & Clark discovered them, no one's idea of country bumpkins. The great white tourists from beyond the shining mountains bartered cleverly and left broke, a custom followed in coastal villages to this day.

In the westward migration that followed (Indian people ignore the big picture and speak of it as invasion and conquest), the wagon road split in southern Idaho. Those immigrants seeking gold, avocados, and film contracts went south to California. Those with their hearts set on rain, dank forests, and lives without hope prodded their oxen to Oregon.

Of these, the ones smart enough to give up settled the fertile inner valleys, carving stump farms from undergrowth and raising families of boring but honest children. The fearless, if not overly bright group that trudged on, weeping and cursing, to the coast found what shelter they could, burned their wagons to stay warm, and reproduced in spite of their misery.

Over the years, each of which seemed like a century, the settlers evolved, in a way, into three much too inbred groups: the pirate clan, the smuggler clan, and the makers of odd things from driftwood and kelp. The culture that endures today, while of morbid interest to anthropologists, isn't for the squeamish.

The Inhabitants Today

It's all well and good, believing there are no bad people. Faith is a virtue. Naivete' is another matter. Confuse the two on the Oregon Coast and life turns ugly fast.

Don't mistake your hosts for the happy natives of National Geographic specials. There'll be no leis and hugs on your arrival, no serenades in the moonlight. You'll be lucky if, when darkness falls, they don't come for you with torches and clam shovels.

These aren't people you should get to know. Or, for that matter, turn your back on. Set aside those warm, fuzzy notions about the family of man. To the water-logged little gnomes peering out from under their rain hoods, you're a visitor from another world: a world of sunlight, laughter, and dry clothes whose existence they know only by rumor and bitterly resent. To them, you're either someone who'll buy driftwood jewelry or can be sold to a crab boat captain with a drinking problem.

Don't bother putting your best foot forward. Your villagers are simply too miserable to care. Nothing you do, not even throwing your life away and joining them, will change things. These are humans who, from the cradle to the grave, never really get warm and dry, and it's fool-ish to think their inner child is somehow nourished by the gloom and damp. It's cruel to suggest to someone wear-ing a ragged tarp and patched gum boots to have a nice day. They know much better than you what sort of day they're going to have, just as surely as they know what the rest of life has in store. They hate their lives, just as you would if you lived here, and being cheery just isn't in them. Your smiles and laughter will grate on their nerves, reminding them that, unlike themselves, you'll soon be going back to a land of sunlight, dry bedding, and meals not involving clams.

These are desperate people whose ancestors settled the Oregon Coast only because they could run no further. If you must venture out among them, keep your money in your boot and your children and pets in sight. Don't lunch in quaint inns that lack a back door. Avoid eye contact with anyone not obviously from out of town, and tell no jokes whose punch line involves eating blubber, luring ships onto reefs, or hiding from the law. If you hire a guide, don't let it lure you onto the beach.

CHAPTER THREE

BASIC TRAVEL TIPS

What Should I Bring?

Any vacation destination (a word you should remember means "place of destiny") has its list of appropriate gear. The Oregon Coast is no exception. As you pack each item into your soon to be lost luggage, ask yourself two questions:

Will this keep me warm and dry?

Will it relieve the mind numbing boredom?

As a general rule, bring nothing you can't leave out in the rain or will miss when it's gone. What the seagulls and raccoons don't carry off, you'll abandon in your eagerness to escape.

Your basic travel kit for the Oregon Coast should include:

1. Professional quality rain gear
2. Rubber boots
3. Thermal underwear
4. A large flashlight that floats
5. A small inflatable raft
6. A powerful rescue beacon
7. Medical records
8. Several books of crossword puzzles
9. Strong antidepressant drugs

Items you needn't bother with:

1. Sunscreen
2. Sunglasses
3. Bathing suit
4. Beach towels
5. Sandals
6. Wiener roasting sticks

What Should I Wear?

Fashion on the Oregon Coast gives new meaning to the word casual. Regional dress leans heavily toward the layered look with flamboyance kept to a minimum. When one dresses with survival in mind, accessorizing fades as a concern.

The most common street ensemble begins with thermal underwear and works its way out to a heavy wool sweater, canvas pants, a sturdy mackinaw, and stout rubber boots. You should bring several flannel shirts for nights on the town and a pair of galoshes for dancing.

If you haven't brought a fun hat, you'll want to buy one. It should be crafted of surprisingly expensive straw or be the sort worn by baseball players. In either case, it should be emblazoned with a tasteless message, the logo of a ruthless corporate sport franchise, or a poor likeness of a pelican, a seagull, or a whale.

How Should I Behave?

You must remember this is your vacation and you're here to have fun. You won't, of course. Coming to the Oregon Coast was the worst blunder of your life. But what's done is done and the sooner you start making the best of things, the sooner it'll be time to leave.

The first rule is not to try to fit in. The gloom and despair around you has been generations in the making and the last thing you want to do is become part of it. Your best approach is to regard the nasty bit of nowhere you've come to as a theme park for the depressed, and the villagers as hired rustics with wet blankets to sell.

Every chance you get, make it clear you deserve far better than what they and their village are dishing up. Sneer often and speak loudly, especially when finding fault. When you can't be condescending or oblivious, laugh gaily over nothing and shout in falsetto to friends on the next block. Encourage your children to be smug, abrasive, and free of both manners and self restraint. This is their vacation too and, unless their innocent pursuit of fun veers

in directions that might involve lawyers, let the little
barbarians run amok. If possible, on roller blades.

CHAPTER FOUR

THINGS THAT LIVE IN THE SEA

Life began in the sea. As miracles go, it was subtle. One day the sun warmed the amino acid froth in some foul smelling tide pool just enough to make DNA curdle out. Had we been watching when it happened, we'd have missed it.

For the next few hundred million years, life mixed and matched itself in the sea without anyone noticing the sort of genetic experiments that were going on. Or, for that matter, raising questions about their wisdom. Most of the experiments were failures and many of the successes were unpleasant.

One day, our amphibian ancestors dragged themselves, flopping and gasping, onto the beach and never looked back. Science assumes they had a reason. An easy explanation is offered by the creatures they left behind.

The Shark

Of the many hostile life forms you'll meet on the Oregon Coast, none should be more scrupulously avoided than the shark. There are no happy shark stories because there are no happy sharks. There are only hungry sharks.

Because sharks have been maiming and eating humans since the beginning of recorded history, much serious attention has been paid to them. Of the great deal we now know, not one bit is encouraging. The story of man meets shark has been, without exaggeration, an unbroken cavalcade of horror. In all the literature, there's not a single mention of anyone running into a shark who was just out looking for a friend. As far as science can tell, a shark wouldn't know a friend if it ate one.

Sharks aren't like the other fish in a very important way: they must move in order to breathe. Marine biologists regard this as a design quirk. Sharks see it as a curse. Being unable to sleep, or even nap, makes the shark unimaginably cranky and its endless pacing gives it an appetite unparalleled in the wild kingdom. The shark's world is divided into two parts: things to eat, and things to tear apart and swallow anyway.

There are only two things to remember about sharks. The first is that they live in the ocean. The second is that they grow to lengths of 30 feet and can snap logs in their teeth. This means you should never venture into the surf wearing anything less than the deck of a large, steel-hulled power launch. Without this, defensive measures will be a humiliating waste of time. Unless the items in your beach bag include a pump action shotgun, cattle prod, and several concussion grenades, your shark will eventually have its way.

Of the many myths surrounding sharks, none is more cruel than the notion that hitting one on the nose with anything smaller than an anvil will shoo it away.

The Octopus

The octopus is a shy creature and your chance of meeting one is small. This is best for all concerned since octopi are the stuff of nightmares: cold eyed, tentacled mollusks who look, for all the world, like aliens from a planet no one visits twice.

The octopus is found, usually by hideous accident, squished into rocky crevices in picturesque tidal pools. Wise travelers will resist the urge to poke it with a stick. Octopi are generally passive, but they can be surprisingly quick, and disentangling even a small one from your face is a wildlife experience you'll wish you'd missed.

Although the octopus seldom attacks without provocation, experience has shown it's hard to tell what might provoke it. If you have the bad luck to find out, panic will be your worst enemy. Your average octopus can be subdued with the baseball bat which you will, if you're smart, be carrying.

Large specimens are another, much more sobering, matter. And large specimens there are. The Oregon Coast offers what can only be called worldclass tentacled mollusks: monstrous, deep sea carnivores worse than your wildest imaginings.

With large octopi, your only chance is to stay out of reach. Unless you're in your motel room, this will pose a challenge. All octopi have a natural talent for fetching. Common sense tells us that, the larger the octopus, the further this talent will reach. Giant octopi can, while completely submerged, snatch you and your toy poodle from the rocks with the lightning ease of a frog catching flies. One moment you're there, the next you're not. As your parrot beaked horror drags you, choking and thrashing, into its lair, you'll wish you'd lingered longer in the kite shop.

The Seal

No animal you'll meet on the Oregon Coast is more adorable than the seal. Seals know this and will play you like a harp. Often called nature's gift to the easily entertained, seals love to bob up next to humans in the surf, bark rudely and applaud themselves. The normal will soon tire of this, as have the locals, who view seals with the same affection others reserve for traveling mime troupes.

Still, marine biologists suspect that if seals didn't exist, the makers of heartwarming nature documentaries would have been forced to invent them. Our fascination doesn't go unrequited. Entire seal families often gather on sand spits to watch migrating humans in pastel beach wear argue with their pups about money.

Endearing as seals are, or are at first, they're not without their dark side. Scholars believe that mermaids, the sirens of sea myth whose beauty lured mariners to a watery grave, were a fantasy inspired by seals, who have nice eyes and love to loll about on reefs. Taking nothing from the seal's natural beauty, comparing even the fairest of them to Daryl Hannah is stark testimony to the loneliness of life at sea.

The Sea Lion

The Oregon Coast is famous for its large sea lion population. The fact that innocent people like you still come points to serious confusion.

Sea lions are not, to begin with, even loosely related to cats. They're close cousins of the dog. And, more importantly, the bear. Walt Disney films aside, the sea lion is a large, amphibious carnivore who won't seem so clumsy and comical when it's bearing down on you like a sumo wrestler with fangs. When this happens, remember that the sea lion's bark, bloodcurdling as it is, is nothing compared to its bite.

It's important to limit your encounters with sea lions to those involving binoculars. Don't think for a moment the huge, tusked beast basking on the rocks is there to bond with you. It's there in spite of you and will behave badly if you forget it. Unless your urge to connect with another species is strong enough to trade a hand and good portion of forearm, never rub a sleeping sea lion behind the ears.

A final note: contrary to what the old villager told you, no one has ever taught a sea lion to fetch by teasing it with a fish.

The Starfish

The starfish is a primitive creature who, in all fairness, is doing the best it can. It seldom seems enough. Aside from agates and seashells, starfish are the most easily collected memento of your day at the beach. The starfish knows this and feels just the way you would about it.

You'd be hard pressed to find a seashore adventure less challenging than stalking the wild starfish. The poor devils move very slowly, when they move at all, a trait that makes them perfect prey for anything bored or hungry enough to bother them. The starfish is just smart enough to know where it stands. It may look calm, even dead, but any starfish you see is running wildly from something, gibbering in terror. Often, it's the memory of being used as a frisbee.

The Sea Anemone

Sea anemones are the ugly green tentacled things in the bottom of the tide pool that look like props from a bad dream.

Anemones are boring to watch but great fun to tease. Small children take special pleasure in prodding them with sticks and squealing with laughter as the anemone, imagining it's going to eat, closes its fleshy tentacles on nothing. The anemone is a very old life form and naturalists doubt seriously it's amused. Unsettling stories continue to surface suggesting that the anemone's days of turning the other tentacle are over.

Evolution on the Oregon Coast has taken many an odd turn, few of them as nasty as the attack anemone. Some villagers swear up and down that attack anemones were here waiting for their great grandparents. Others insist they're a new species that evolved in response to being teased. It hardly matters. Your only concern will be not to mistake one kind from another, an ability you could be the first to master.

Aside from its stubborn refusal to ignore insult, the only characteristics that set the attack anemone apart are its startling quickness and total lack of mercy. Prod one of these simple life forms with your sand shovel; it snatches it from your hands and beats you senseless.

As you sink to your knees in the tide pool, trying vainly to ward off the blows, it'll be too late to remember that anemones are neither plants nor vegetarians.

The Clam

The clam is, bless its heart, the only creature on the Oregon Coast more boring than the starfish. Technically speaking, clams are bivalve mollusks closely related to rocks. In lay terms, clams are snails without the excitement.

Clams spend their entire lives buried under the sand. For this reason alone, thoughtful visitors will avoid the clam watching tours offered by villagers with no sense of shame. As opposed to a whale, your clam will never breach the surface so you can catch it in the little net they sold you. If you're lucky, a small hole in the sand will bubble. And the villagers, bless their hearts, will dance and clap their hands.

The Crab

Crabs are large underwater insects who, after millions of years of painstaking evolution, have managed to become uglier than an octopus. It would be wrong to suppose they make up for things with a pleasing personality. As many a vacationer has discovered, crabs aren't armor plated for nothing.

It's hard to say anything about crabs without sounding mean spirited and unfair. Still, the truth remains. Crabs, at their absolute best, are bottom feeding sea bugs whose place in the natural order depends on something like you washing up in the surf. When push comes to shove, and it will, crabs are nasty little scuttlers whose fondest dreams involve their pincers and your soft body parts.

It's important that, while on the beach, you appear neither dead nor disabled. You may not see them but the crabs are there, watching from the ripples with their disgusting little periscope eyes, waiting for the moment you lie down on your overpriced beach towel. Under no circumstances, close your eyes. Crabs on the Oregon Coast move quickly, are quiet as ghosts, and work well in groups.

One final word of warning. If your stay is longer than twelve hours, a crab festival will take place near you. You must let it take place without you. There are reasons villagers on the Oregon Coast make offerings to the crab people and you don't want to know them. You especially don't want to be chosen crab king or crab queen and spend the last of your holiday staked out in a tide pool.

The Sea Serpent

It would be foolish to let wild rumors of sea serpents dampen your vacation fun. Granted, for many centuries, men sober and responsible enough to be trusted with large sailing ships have reported nightmarish encounters with prehistoric monsters from the deep. The truth still remains: not one of these eye witness accounts has withstood the scrutiny of modern science. Of course, neither has the bumblebee's reputed ability to fly.

The important thing to remember about sea serpents is that they live in the sea. As long as you don't go into the ocean, or near it, the chance you'll be torn apart and eaten by something that no longer inhabits the planet is small. Except during full moons and certain low tides when imaginary dinosaurs the size of dirigibles clamber ashore to feed. Then it won't matter where you are.

Your best approach is philosophical. Things are what they are and all the worrying in the world won't change them. You'll either meet a sea serpent or you won't. Go about your fun as if there were nothing to fear, keeping a weather eye out for large wakes and your ear tuned to the sort of earth shaking screech an amphibious tyrannosaurus might make. Should the unthinkable occur, try to take photographs.

CHAPTER FIVE

THINGS THAT PROWL THE LAND

It's important not to allow the dreadful judgment that brought you here to spill over into your dealings with local wildlife. Unless you spend your vacation locked inside your RV (an idea that will seem less silly as the days drag on), you'll encounter many animals normally associated with wildlife parks. These encounters will give you new appreciation for cyclone fencing and tear gas.

The Deer

The rain forests of the Oregon Coast were once abound, quite literally, with deer. The coming of the repeating rifle and the off-road family assault vehicle, coupled with unlimited supplies of cheap whisky and ammunition have changed the picture somewhat. Any deer you see within a day's walk of the village will be shell shocked, suicidal, or seeking sanctuary in a local church.

It's the deer you don't see that should concern you. The lopsided fun of hunting season hasn't been lost on these shy forest creatures. Nimble, fleet of foot, and sporting antlers that can gut a grizzly, deer on the Oregon Coast have become masters of the ambush.

Be wary of fauns bleating their hearts out in small clearings. They'll only be bait. Just before your hand nuzzles that cute little nose, Bambi will spring several feet into the air and do a tap dance on your forehead. At which point, the forest will explode with the thundering hoof beats of your karma. The deer think of this as leveling the playing field.

The Elk

The elk is basically a deer on steroids, large specimens reaching the size of Clydesdales. They would be, even without antlers that are to the deer's what the broadsword is to the pen knife, creatures well worth avoiding.

As long as you stay indoors or on brightly lit streets, the odds are good no elk will bother you. Stray into the forest and you belong to them. A bit of wildlife lore your brochure fails to mention is the bull elk's talent for using its antlers, often measuring five feet across, like a lacrosse racquet. Tournament class elk have been observed playing catch with their prey for hours before finishing the job with a stampede.

The Bear

Everything you've heard about bears is true, and then some. Should you be foolish enough to go into the forest, or onto your porch, make certain you're not standing between a bear and its cub. Or, for that matter, between a bear and anything. It's often possible to frighten a bear away by beating on pots and pans and yelling shoo. Other times, it just pushes them over the edge. But then, you came for adventure and know all about this.

The Raccoon

No forest creature is more comical than the raccoon. This gives them an edge they hardly need. Raccoons are close relatives of the panda, or teddy, bear. This is a source of endless embarrassment to the panda since raccoons are nimble fingered delinquents much too smart for their own good.

Whatever else you say about them, raccoons are gifted thieves. Because of the black mask, they're often taken for furry little forest Zorros. The confusion seldom lasts long. Zorro stole from the rich and gave to the poor. Racoons steal anything that' s not nailed down and keep it.

As birds are born to fly, raccoons are born to burgle. For the average raccoon (and you'll find most raccoons are far above average), locked cars and chained trash cans are a diversion, not a challenge. Few precautions, certainly not storm windows and dead bolts, are beyond the skills of a determined family of raccoons who will, when the mood strikes, rip through the roof of your quaint rental cabin to get at the hot dogs and marshmallows. Naturalists agree that if the raccoons and crows ever get together, the game will be pretty much over.

The Mountain Lion

The moutain lions who live on the Oregon coast are, with one exception, no different than mountain lions anywhere: large, incredibly nimble carnivores who may or may not decide to drag you down and eat you. The ones who live in the rain forest are just miserable and wet to boot.

The Sasquatch

The sasquatch, or bigfoot, is a hairy, eight foot tall humanoid who probably doesn't exist. They probably don't exist in the Himalayas either where, for centuries, the easily fooled have called them 'yeti', or abominable snowmen. Whether the yeti is, by nature, more abominable than a sasquatch is a subject of spirited debate among people you should avoid.

If sasquatches do exist, the fact they're so seldom seen has prompted many to assume they're shy and harmless. It might also mean they avoid us as religiously as we avoid lawyers and sociopaths. Some sasquatches certainly don't sound shy and harmless in the eye witness accounts where they roll boulders down on campgrounds and flatten oil drums in their bare hands. But there's probably nothing to this.

For whatever reason, the sasquatch lives in the most remote reaches of the rain forest and the chance you'll meet one is quite small. Nearly nonexistent. Unless, as the stories go, sasquatches enjoy the occasional night on the beach. And hunt humans down for sport. And drag them back to their caves and make love slaves of them. This is probably pure poppycock.

CHAPTER SIX

THINGS THAT FLY THROUGH THE AIR

When your visit to the Oregon Coast is finally over, you'll carry many memories back to the real world. None will be harder to erase than your encounters with local bird life. Given common sense and a good pith helmet, they needn't result in permanent injury.

What you need to remember about birds is that, like alligators, they're directly descended from dinosaurs. Birds are winged reptiles whose ancestors were vicious predators who stood thirty feet at the shoulder and moved like greased lightning. No bird has forgotten its days at the top of the food chain and neither should you.

The Seagull

The seagull is the king of coastal birddom. Not, as the unwary soon learn, by virtue of its natural nobility, but because the seagull is a large bird and there are mil lions of them.

As long as you keep your wits about you, wear a catcher's mask and overcoat and carry a tennis racket, you'll be fine. Villagers love to spin tales of small children and medium sized dogs snatched from the beach and carried off to sea by laughing bands of gulls. This almost never happens. Most seagulls are content to demand food on the sidewalk, hurtle through plate glass windows, and pose for sofa-sized paintings. Verified seagull horror stories aren't nearly as common since the villagers began carrying scatter guns. The few documented tragedies would never have happened if the humans involved had just put down their muffins and backed away.

What you must accept about seagulls is this: whatever they want will be theirs in the end. If you hand over your food without grumbling, they'll go back to blocking your path, shredding your designer kite, and making poo on your colorful hat. You'll discover that seagulls make poo with deadly accuracy and aren't above vendetta.

As long as you have nothing they want, most seagulls will leave you alone. Of course, this being the Oregon Coast, you can expect the occasional psychotic break. The odd gull who, friends will say later, had been keeping too much to himself. Brooding, perhaps, over the good old days. For whatever reason, something snaps, and the berserk gull of your karma dives out of the fog, shrieking like a banshee, beats you senseless with its wings and pecks your vital organs to a pulp. Then it will take your muffin.

The Crow

The crow is common to many parts of the world. It lives on the Oregon Coast with grudging permission from the seagulls. This makes the crow try harder, an incentive it hardly needs, and consumes it with bitterness and lust for revenge.

As any bird watcher will tell you, crows are smart as whips, an evolutionary success story gone badly awry. The world would be a better place if the crow applied its intelligence to good works. Sadly for all concerned, crows prefer to wile away the hours slouched on roof beams and power lines, waiting for the moment you leave your RV unlocked or your cinnamon roll unattended.

Any crow you see has an agenda you don't want to be part of. If you'd rather your holiday didn't turn into something it'll take years to laugh about, never forget that 1) crows are congenital thieves, 2) they've nothing but time on their hands, and 3) the dullest among them is more than a match for the cleverest member of your party.

Unlike other birds who take food because they're hungry, crows steal for the joy that's in it. Solitary crows may be bought off with your sunglasses, wristwatch, or an interesting set of ear rings. Crows in groups tend to egg each other on. To describe a flock of crows as a nuisance is to barely scratch the truth. In less time than it takes to buy your little bag of salt water taffy, a raiding party of crows can strip your minivan to its axles. They don't do it for the parts. They do it to show the seagulls they can.

The Sandpiper

The Oregon Coast is filled with unpleasant surprises, the sandpiper being high on the list. The motley little tweeters careening along the tide line are cute for a reason. Clawing out a living among seagulls and crows has taught them to be endearing and quick. They're also anything but stupid.

The first rule in dealing with sandpipers is to disregard appearances. They are, strictly speaking, snipes: a Latin term meaning 'small bird with crazy temper'. Like all birds, they were once dinosaurs too and their comically reduced circumstances have turned them into twisted little thugs with the eyes of an eagle and the compassion of a cobra. They're also short tempered and insanely eager to strike the first blow.

Because sandpipers are constantly underfoot, your encounters with them will usually boil down to futile attempts to fend them off. One on one, the average sandpiper poses little threat to an adult in good physical condition. Unless the twittering little psychopath darts up your pant leg, at which point you'll be glad you remembered your ball peen hammer. Roving bands of sand snipes are another, less happy story. Sooner or later they'll surround you and, when you've run out of bread crumbs, that will be that.

CHAPTER SEVEN

THE NATIVE PLANTS AND YOU

Kelp

Of the many ghastly mistakes made by visitors to the Oregon Coast, few are more common than taking kelp for granted. Villagers will look you straight in the eye and tell you the long, bulbous sea plant is harmless; just a make believe bullwhip for the children. When you turn your back, they'll slap their knees and snort.

In its undersea garden, kelp bothers no one. Why should it? The tide comes in, the tide goes out, life is good. Left to itself, kelp hasn't a mean fiber in its slimy green body. It's only when the forces of nature rip it out by its roots and fling it onto a beach lined with humans in pastel beach wear that kelp turns murderous.

Laughing at the idea of being attacked by a plant is much easier than laughing at the reality. What the villagers don't tell you, and what your brochures aren't about to mention, is that kelp jumps. Keep your pets on a short leash, encourage children to walk in pairs and to blow their police whistle before the kelp starts dragging them toward the surf.

The Tree

Much has been written about the ancient forests of the Oregon Coast. This is good since, for all practical purposes, they're gone. On the bright side, the few patches remaining are sometimes visible from the highway and are open most weekends. Admission varies depending on the size of the stumps. There's an extra charge for the chain saw demonstrations and reservations are advised.

Mold and Fungus

It's common for first time visitors to the Oregon Coast to mistake the rain forest for the trees. In reality, the region's dominant plant forms are mold and fungus: simple organisms that thrive in the dank conditions found in neglected refrigerators. This makes the spot you've chosen for your vacation one vast petri dish.

It's safe to say any memories you have of your holiday will be associated with the smell of mildew. All surfaces, including human skin, not constantly swept with a blow dryer are soon covered with thriving colonies of mold. To say mildew takes over quickly is an understatement bordering on insult. Unless you're a professional exterminator, beating back the slime mold with cleaning solvents and propane torches will eventually dampen your fun.

If you stay longer than a weekend, your belongings will be reduced to shapeless mounds of rot. What few articles that escape will smell so foul you'll burn them. Complaining will accomplish nothing. The villagers no longer notice the rank vapors in the shower or the furry coating on the walls. They couldn't and still go on.

Pound for pound, mildew is king of the rain forest, but free standing fungi are nearly as rampant. Biologists hesitate even to guess how many varieties of mushrooms and toadstools make their home on the Oregon Coast. Many of them suspect, however, it's only a matter of time before the spongy mammoths eat what trees the loggers couldn't get to.

Excitement is a scarce resource here. Of the many local celebrations you'll want to avoid, none is sadder or more unnerving than the fungus festival. Each spring and autumn, driven by primal urges you don't want to know about, the villagers gather in clearings with pick axes and shovels. For hours they just stand in the rain, muttering and giggling and poking each other, and swilling heaven knows what from their kelp gourds.

Critical mass is eventually achieved. A bell is rung (or, more commonly, a cast iron stew pot is whacked with a mallet) and the poor wretches race into the woods with crude carts to drag back old growth mushrooms and vile, tumorous looking masses hacked from rotten logs.

Competition is fierce and prizes of shiny pebbles and bits of bright colored yarn are awarded for the largest non-deadly specimens. The award ceremony is followed, first by fist fights, then by several hours of morose chanting and clacking of clam shells. When the rain has put out the last of the fires, the natives squat in the mud, gnaw on their fungus, and weep.

CHAPTER EIGHT

ACTIVITIES AND ADVENTURES

Many activities and adventures await you on the Oregon Coast. Many others lurk. Given sensible precautions, and the sort of luck reserved for fools and children, you can emerge from most of them shaken but intact. Your holiday will be much like sailing: hours of mind numbing boredom punctuated with bouts of stark terror. You won't be coming back to the Oregon Coast, but you'll never forget you were here.

Sightseeing

The Oregon Coast is one of the most beautiful spots on the planet. Sadly, it won't be visible through the fog and rain.

Your first vacation discovery will be that you've been badly duped. The dazzling four color photos in your brochure are either outright fakes or were taken during a freak break between storm fronts. Unless your visit coincides with a similar miracle, the driving sleet and ground clouds will make scenic glimpses of anything beyond arm's length cause for surprise. One doesn't discover the Oregon Coast, one stumbles over it. Prudent sightseers stay in groups and rope themselves together.

Because nothing discourages a nature walk quite like rain that blows sideways, your exploring will be confined to the many roadside attractions thrown up in a desperate attempt to get your money. Aside from the 'Crab Pits of Mystery' and 'Clam World', both of which are worth avoiding, the Oregon Coast has many depressing museums displaying evidence of the suffering and despair visited on those who came a little too far west. Bits of broken plows, bullet-riddled whiskey ladles, the occasional scrap from a sealskin bridal dress. Not much, certainly not hopes and dreams, lasts long in a climate tailor made for rust and mold.

Deep Sea Fishing

Deep sea fishing off the Oregon Coast is a once in a lifetime experience you should definitely decide against. A quick glance at the insurance premiums paid by those who fish the North Pacific more than tells the tale. These are professional fishermen who risk death in order to eat. Charter boat crews risk death because people like you will pay big money for the chance to die with them.

If you've set your sights on adventure but aren't committed to burial at sea, you should pick your charter boat carefully. Your captain should not have a faraway look in his eye, drink rum from the bottle, or have more than two artificial limbs. Before any money changes hands, insist on seeing the boat and meeting the crew. The boat should have a motor rather than oars and the crew should not be gnawing at their restraints.

Since there are no adequate protective measures for the holiday lark you've signed on for, you'll need little in the way of personal gear: strong tranquilizers, a lucky charm perhaps, a concealed firearm to level the playing field when the inevitable mutiny breaks out. And, of course, your cold water flotation suit which, when the Pequod goes down like a stone, may extend your life for as long as forty minutes.

But enough of the dark side. Until the disasters start unfolding, you're going to have the fishing experience of your life. As you strap yourself into the chest harness and the crew starts reeling out the 1,000 lb. test line attached to the oil drums, remember there are things that live in the North Pacific you should pray you don't catch.

Local Festivals

Your guidebook, written and published by people who vacation elsewhere, will list scores of local festivals. The festivals will have quaint names: Clam Days, Crab Roundup, the Kelp and Beer Bake. You'll regret so much as driving by any of them.

Those festivals not canceled because the host village disappeared in the last storm will be gloomy affairs characterized by group weeping, the singing of morbid sea chanties, and the drinking of mushroom beer. The drinking of mushroom beer is inevitably followed by octopus wrestling and crab tossing. Or crab wrestling and octopus tossing. Regardless how many are in your group, you must be gone before any of this begins.

Hiking

Your brochures will go on at great length about the joys of hiking the Oregon Coast. Unless you're a seasoned survivalist, this is absolute nonsense. No one 'hikes' on the Oregon Coast. They scurry from one bit of shelter to the next. Visitors who, lulled by a brief break in the downpour, set off gaily into the rainforest soon learn the sort of nature they're communing with.

If your holiday isn't being sponsored by the Discovery Channel, never venture from your mini van without storm gear, a powerful lantern, marine flares, and a three day ration of jerky. Do not, for any reason, stray from the path. The rough tracks hacked through the dripping undergrowth of poison oak, thorny vines, and mushrooms the size of haystacks are there for a reason, and striking out on a shortcut could be your last bad decision. The rainforests of the Oregon Coast are filled with the dim cries of those who trusted their brochures.

Walks on the beach are just as foolish. Trained rescue teams are routinely lost in the fog. Should you be idiot enough to join them, your kit should include a Coast Guard approved flotation vest. As you stumble blindly along, your only clue as to where the ocean is will be the murderous pounding of the surf and the muffled cries of your fellow nitwits caught by freak waves. Sadly, all sound will be drowned out by the howling winds. Rope the family together, keep your eye on your compass, and avoid veering west.

Beach Combing

Beach combing on the Oregon Coast quickly deteriorates into following your footprints back to warmth and shelter. It would never occur to a normal person to stop and gather bits of flotsam and jetsam along the way. But then, beach combers aren't normal people to begin with.

Just as some of us are born to whittle sticks and hum to ourselves, others are born to comb beaches. Beach combing is more than an activity, it's a calling, a random genetic trait: an odd roll of the DNA dice that, instead of making someone collect bits of brightly colored ribbon, drives them to wander the tide line and giggle over what's washed up. As F. Scott Fitzgerald said of the rich, beach combers aren't like you and me. They're not even like the other villagers.

As you set off down the beach, keep the truth firmly in mind. Behind the bells and whistles of civilization, humans are still hunter gatherers at heart. Female humans on holiday at the shore hunt and gather in galleries and shops. Or, whenever possible, shoppes. Male humans hunt and gather in manly places as far from the females as possible. Some of them just don't come back.

Male or female, its naive to laugh, believing you're somehow above it all. Don't think for a minute the bearded rustics with the driftwood staffs and sealskin tote bags were always as you see them now. Their eyes haven't always shone that way. They didn't always dance around battered crab pots shouting gibberish, or grow up dreaming of the day they'd be local color. The poor devils just combed the beach a little too far. One day the stars lined up, their DNA dealt them a new hand and, in terms of a meaningful life, they were gone.

Clam Digging

Clam digging is, as you'll quickly discover, not what the person who sold you the lucky bucket and shovel promised. It's not, to begin with, even vaguely romantic. No activity in the world cries out less for champagne and violins than burrowing in the muck on your hands and knees looking for a primitive creature who's gone to great lengths to avoid you.

There's nothing about the relationship between humans and clams that any of us should be proud of. Evidently, somewhere in our desperate past, food was scarce enough to make a large brained hominid stoop to eating what amounts to the internal organs of a rock. Necessity is sometimes the mother of embarrassment. Over the next few millenia, most hominids learned from the experience, vowed to better themselves as a species, and moved on. Isolated pockets remain. To this day, hominids on the Oregon Coast continue to use clams to ruin potato soup.

Regardless where you stand on eating something

58

nature clearly intended for seagulls and otters, the heady mix of salt sea air and unspeakable boredom will drive you, shovel in hand, to a fog shrouded beach at low tide. Silly, but there it is. In a matter of minutes, you'll discover that much of the misery of clam digging springs from its total lack of excitement. It was no accident that Hemingway never once considered writing 'The Old Man and the Clam'. There's only so much you can say about shoveling sand in the rain.

As your native guide spins tales of the great clam hunts of its youth, remember these are people who stalk starfish and invented the world's only mushroom trap. Clam digging involves no epic struggle between man and mollusk. Your prey will just be lying there, waiting in the sand. So, unfortunately, are the king clams.

King clams, which you can bet aren't mentioned in your brochure, are to ordinary clams what boulders are to beach pebbles. With one important difference: unlike actual boulders, king clams have an appetite matched only by their patience. And their faith that low tide will bring them something to eat. Something that actually digs a hole to get to it. If, while digging, your shovel seems stuck, don't try to free it with your hands.

Camping

One hesitates even to discuss camping on the Oregon Coast. Unless your idea of a vacation includes clinging to life until the helicopters reach you, your first vacation rule should be never to sleep anywhere that lacks storm windows and room service. People who live here work themselves to an early grave stacking plank upon plank in a vain attempt to ward off the elements. And you've come here to camp. One wonders whether to laugh or cry.

Simply put, your travel agent lied. There is no joy in camping here, only grim satisfaction should you survive what will seem like a bad chapter from a Jack London novel. Nothing in the way of protective gear will save you from weather more foul than you can imagine. As your other guide book forgot to mention, the Oregon Coast offers twenty-eight different varieties of rain.

Before so much as considering a camp out, sit down with the family and ask some serious questions. Did you really come all this way to huddle in the darkness, soaked to the bone, listening to the wind shred your Everest-rated dome tent like a cheap sail? Will the camp songs and marshmallows be the same without a fire and dry clothes? When the seagulls and raccoons come for the last of the cheese crackers, will you stand together or fall apart?

Swimming

As you thumb through your fantasy filled brochures, look closely at the photos of happy vacationers frolicking in the surf. Are any of them actually swimming? Of course not. In the icy waters of the North Pacific, swimming is the last desperate act of someone who's been washed from the boat. Once in the water, survival time is measured in minutes, not fun filled hours.

As any map will show you, the Oregon Coast is much closer to the Aleutian Islands than it is to Bali. This explains why the children in the photos are running from the surf rather than toward it. Nor are their smiles what they seem. They're either screaming or have been stricken with facial rictus, the painful muscle contractions that signal the end game of hypothermia. Local inhabitants devote much effort to making sure they never have to swim. You should do the same.

Sunbathing

The author refuses even to discuss the notion of sun-
bathing.

Surfing

The beaches of Oregon offer magnificent surfing opportunities for both novice and advanced lunatics. The waves of the north coast are especially spectacular and deadly: crashing walls of foam and tree trunks moving at the speed of a freight train. Beneath the waves, boulders the size of Volkswagens roll across the sea floor like marbles.

Don't listen to villagers with surfboards to rent. Nothing about surfing on the Oregon Coast will remind you of Mexico or Maui. Those are tropical beaches with sunlight, balmy breezes, and fruit drinks. Here, there's only horizontal rain, wind chill, and the occasional Coast

Guard helicopter. People who've surfed the world over literally surf the world over before coming to the North Pacific. They can't all be ignorant sissies.

As you paddle through the two-story swells, shivering uncontrollably in your wet suit, waiting for the murderous mountain of water that will reduce your surf board to splintered driftwood and you to a small news item, remember two things: you were supposed to be having fun and there are things in the ocean that will eat you.

Generations of not being stalked and dragged down by species other than our own has made us complacent. Nothing cures complacence faster than being eaten alive, and nothing in nature is there for you more than the shark.

As you bob on your surfboard, trying desperately to stay alive, your little arms stroking, your little flippers flailing away, you'll look, to the shark, very much like a seal. Or a sea lion. Or sea turtle. In the end, it won't matter. Sharks on the Oregon Coast grow to the size of cargo canoes and routinely swallow anchors.

Wind Surfing

This is nothing short of madness. Travel agents with tickets to sell, and villagers with sail boards to rent, will tell you the Oregon Coast is a wind surfer's dream come true. They'll be lying through their teeth.

'Wind' isn't the word to describe the colossal movements of air you'll experience here, often indoors. Wind is something one spits into, races with, or seeks shelter from. Wind is something to be allowed for, dealt with, or at least lived through. Wind on the Oregon Coast carries off livestock, uproots trees, and carves mountains in front of your eyes.

Should you opt to ignore reason and hoist your gaily colored little sail, be prepared to go very fast and not be back soon. Many wind surfing endurance records have been set in the North Pacific, most of them unintentionally. Freighter crews and air/sea rescue personnel are continually amazed how far a sail boarder with a strong will to live can travel before dehydration and hypothermia end the fun.

Log Bobbing

Life on the Oregon Coast breeds desperate amusements, the most suicidal among them being log bobbing. Riding logs in the surf is a local tradition dating back to those first miserable years when pioneers without hope gathered on the beach to drink homemade beer and court death.

Log bobbing is, in spirit, a close cousin of sand diving: a dependably fatal activity involving home made beer, windswept headlands, and bungee cords of braided kelp. Considered as sport, a mistake the sane don't make twice, log bobbing brings together the worst elements of bull wrestling, tree catching, and high impact drowning.

In keeping with the intelligence level of those involved, the rules of log bobbing are simple. One climbs onto a log tossing wildly in the surf and tries not to fall off and die. As with any blood sport, there are skill levels to log bobbing only a fool would ignore.

Novice log bobbers should not, as a rule, bob on logs longer than they are tall or thicker through than their waist. The log will still maim you but, given decent karma and a good set of lungs, you may still crawl away alive. It's important not to let your log come to rest on top of you.

Until you get the hang of things, wear a brightly colored helmet and your medic alert tag. Should the inevitable happen, tethering a helium filled balloon to your welded steel rib cage protector will make you much easier to find.

Log bobbing at tournament level is something you shouldn't even watch: a grim, sudden death affair involving thundering breakers and water soaked trees, slick as greased eels and weighing several tons. Those veteran log bobbers still able to move their lips will tell you no moment in sport compares to feeling the waves rise over your nostrils as a tree trunk crushes your long bones. Strictly speaking, they'll be right.

Kite Flying

Owing to the savage gales that constantly lash the Oregon Coast, no beach activity is more dependable, or stupid, than flying a kite. If you haven't brought your own, something clever and colorful can be found at a kite shop in the village, often for less than the price of a good used car. The wind will quickly tear it to pieces.

Through bouts of trial and error too terrible to describe, villagers have learned not to bother with flimsy, high tech designs, opting instead for personal wind craft constructed of heavy canvas and galvanized pipe. The last thing you'll need is kite string. Kite flying on the Oregon Coast calls for braided hemp lanyards, steel snap rings, and several hundred feet of logging chain.

You won't need to race up and down the beach try-ing to get your kite to take off. Short of throwing your-self onto it, something you shouldn't do, there'll be noth-ing you can do to stop it. If conditions are right, or wrong, you'll soon discover hang gliding. Those vacationers who suffer from vertigo, or who wish to see their loved ones again, should resist the temptation to fasten their chain to their life jacket.

Bicycling

Your trip to the Oregon Coast won't be complete until you and every member of your party over the age of three rent bicycles to ride on the beach. Nothing could be more ill advised. With the possible exception of ice skates, no form of transportation is less suited to sand than the bicycle.

Given average intelligence, you'll realize your mistake very quickly. And, since you've rented the bicycles for the day, your only option will be to ride them through the village at speeds sufficient to achieve the fun you've paid for. No matter if you haven't ridden a bicycle in years, or possess a natural lack of balance. This is, after all, your vacation and you deserve a little madcap misadventure. Any villager who can't leap out of your way is probably defective and needs to be culled from the herd. Besides, you'll be leaving soon and will never see any of them again.

71

Horseback Riding

A quick look at a map will tell you the wild west goes no further than the Oregon Coast. Neither does anyone riding a horse. You should keep this in mind as you and your rented steed canter on the beach at sunset.

What the cackling little gnomes at the stable didn't tell you is that, like the humans who live here, the horses of the Oregon Coast are at the end of their rope. Years spent trudging through the mud and downpour with overweight tourists on their back can make ending it all with a headlong gallop into the surf seem like perfectly good sense. The chance to take you with them is just frosting on the cake.

Don't be fooled by appearances. The large and not too bright animal you're sitting on isn't docile, it's morose. There is no bright side to its life, it knows things aren't going to get any better, and your cheery giddyup could well be the straw that breaks its will to go on. You must be sure you're not trotting on a headland at the time.

Building Sand Castles

Because you're on holiday at the seashore, you'll feel a restless, childlike urge to build a sand castle. Nothing good will come of it. Unlike other beaches you might have picked, building sand castles on the Oregon Coast means exposing yourself to the elements. And, just as importantly, to roving bands of sand crabs that scour the surf like piranhas.

By way of equipment, you'll need only a bucket and shovel. Any bucket and shovel will do but, because you're on holiday, you'll want to buy expensive and easily broken ones in one of the quaint village shops that specialize in robbing you blind. They should be made of gaily colored plastic in order to show up dimly in the snapshots your friends will regret you took. Your only other

74

need will be sand, small bags of which are sold to the gullible on every street corner.

The first rule in sand castle construction is to begin simply and set your sights low. Throwing yourself into a scale model of Versailles will only lead to heartache when the tide comes in. Not to worry. Your bucket shaped mounds with their crude walls and towers and little pretend roads will, before you know it, take on a life their own, blossoming into something which, given feverish imagination and several quarts of beer, looks almost like a castle made inexpertly from sand.

Tsunami Watching

If you plan to leave the Oregon Coast alive, you'll want to make tsunami watching a constant seashore activity. Granted, by the time you see a tsunami, there's precious little to be done, but the few eye witness accounts say they're really something to watch.

Tsunamis are often called tidal waves. This is seriously misleading. Tsunamis have nothing to do with tides. Tsunamis have to do with destiny. Much, much more than large waves, tsunamis are breathtaking special effects: towering, Cecil B. DeMille walls of water crashing ashore out of nowhere like the hand of an angry god.

As opposed to waves associated with hurricanes and typhoons, there is no high season for tsunamis. There's also not a low one, or a less likely time of day or night for what the media will call a sobering natural disaster. Tsunamis are triggered by undersea earthquakes, a fact that makes them classic random events. Or, if you prefer, acts of God. The twitching of the earth's crust that triggers the tsunami with your name on it could have happened on the ocean floor hours ago and a thousand miles away. Unless your beach kit includes sophisticated seismic equipment, your tsunami will come as a complete surprise.

While individual tsunamis are wildly unpredictable, there's a disturbing overall pattern. Excavations of buried settlements show that beach front on the Oregon Coast slips under the waves, like clockwork, every three centuries or so. Geologists call these episodes "sudden submergence events". Historians call the effects "destruction of Biblical proportions". One minute there's human habitation, the next moment there's not.

By a nasty coincidence, the last of these sudden submergence events happened about three centuries ago, making last week the safest time to visit the Oregon Coast for the next few decades.

Shopping

Hours of mindless fun awaits you in the village shops, especially if you've recently come into great wealth. If you're not someone who spends large blocks of time looking for tax shelters, and aren't taking powerful prescription drugs, purchasing anything during your stay will lead to anger and stark disbelief.

Regardless how many native marketplaces you've

bargained your way through, the Oregon Coast will come as an unpleasant surprise. At some point as you browse among the sofa sized seascapes, driftwood door stops, and imported souvenir baseball caps, you'll wonder just how stupid these people think you are. This will be both wrong and unfair. The villagers don't think you're stupid. They think you're rich and they want your money. Remember that, to them, you're someone who's paid more than they've ever seen to visit a place they can't afford to leave.

In any personal encounter that involves money, which is to say any encounter you're likely to have, don't expect to be cut any slack. These are villagers with baskets to sell and you're someone the gods have sent to buy them at any price. They may be dull, but they're not stupid. They know that extravagance is part of your fun and spare no effort dreaming up ways for you to spend like a drunken sailor.

Everything you see will be astonishingly overpriced. Mostly out of naked greed, but partly due to the very real isolation of the Oregon Coast. Any object here, including food and clothing, was either hauled in over the mountains or washed up on the beach.

Every region, no matter how bleak, has its unique native crafts. Persia has its carpets, Mexico its silver work, California its screen tests. The Oregon Coast is known the world over for its driftwood doorstops, clam shell jewelry, and car deodorizers of macramed kelp.

Promenading

Should the rain ever let up, you'll be tempted to join your fellow displaced persons in a promenade through the village. Promenading mustn't be confused with taking a walk. Promenading involves the need to be noticed and success depends largely on overdressing. Wear nothing that's not new, clearly expensive, and glaringly out of place. If you must dress down, do so in ways calculated to startle and offend.

As you saunter along the boardwalk, your posture and gait, your every bored and offhand gesture must tell the world who you are: a member of the vacationing class whose destiny is to be admired and entertained. Adopt an air of amused contempt, as if nothing and no one measures up. This being the Oregon Coast, nothing and no one will. Cultivate the sneer, the pout, and the arched eyebrow. Failing these, adopt a blank stare. Above all, be oblivious. Idle imperiously in doorways, block the sidewalk whenever possible, and give way to no one whose credit line isn't longer than your own.

If you haven't brought a dog, you must arrange to borrow or rent one. Nothing sets one apart quite like holding the reins of a matching brace of mastiffs as they clear your way on the footpath. If great danes and wolfhounds are beyond your rental agreement, opt for one of the smaller, psychotic breeds that lunge at anything larger than themselves.

Night Life

Unless you find yourself in a city (and, this being the Oregon Coast, you won't) there will be no night life. There'll scarcely be a day life. It's not from ignorance that those who vacation in Mexico, Florida, or the Lesser Antilles, don't vacation here. In those other places, there are bright lights, many of them neon. There are restaurants and nightclubs filled with people enjoying themselves: dining, dancing, being warm and dry. There's fun in those places, or at least a fair chance for it. The Oregon Coast lacks so much as its hint.

The place you've come to isn't the end of the world. It is, however, the miserable wind-whipped edge of it. There are roads, many of them graveled regularly, and mail service. Most days, there'll be electricity. Aside from this, even loose comparisons to civilization inland fall hopelessly apart.

To those who live here, night life consists of bun

dling the family under oilskin tarps and praying for the dawn. It would never cross their minds to slog through the howling winds and downpour to meet friends for pasta. Their friends (to whom pasta is 'noodles') are busy anyway, huddling around a seaweed fire cursing their existence. If the gloomy little hamlet you're stranded in is especially lively, there may be lights showing after dark. They'll be coming from one of three places.

1. A much too rustic pub named after a pelican, a sea gull, or a whale. There'll be a faded wooden sign over the door, lit by a storm lantern, bashing itself to splinters in the gale force winds. Inside, morose villagers with nothing left to lose will be drinking heavily, throwing darts at each other, and challenging strangers to leg wrestle. The bartender will be edgy, have bulging forearms and be carrying a ball bat. There may be food. There won't be a menu or an interesting vinaigrette.

Don't drink the house wine, eat anything stored in large

pickle jars (especially if there are tentacles), or engage in conversation with anyone carrying a harpoon. While you wait out the rain, sit quietly with your back to the door, make eye contact with no one, and avoid showing fear.

2. A resort motel named after a pelican, a sea gull, or a whale. There'll be a restaurant and lounge featuring historic red velour booths and storm windows looking out on the fog. There'll be a fireplace but the wood will be too wet to burn. The staff will be young, friendly, and saving their tips for an escape to Fiji. The television will be on but the cable will be out.

The background music will lean heavily to Wagner, sad songs of the sea, or the sort of soft rock associated with black velvet paintings. On weekends there may be live music. It will be performed by the crew of a crab boat who'll have been drinking since early morning.

3. A late night diner named after the original owner who will have died from the effects of strong drink. The lighting will be mercifully dim and your wait person will be Betty or Nadine, both of whom are older than dirt and have seen all they need to of life. There'll be several villagers at the counter, every one of them the bitter victim

of some horrible personal tragedy. The wise visitor will make no attempt to draw them out. The menu will be short and to the point, the fare much too home made, and the "special" something dragged up from the beach and deep fried. There'll be a soup of the day. It will be clam chowder. Don't ask for a latte, or a list of herbal teas. Betty and Nadine have lifetimes of experience dealing with people like you.

GLOSSARY OF USEFUL PHRASES

No guidebook would be complete without a glossary of often used phrases. You might think that, since English is the native tongue, you'd have no difficulty making yourself understood. But then, you thought this would be a good place to spend your vacation.

Please help me, I am cold and wet.
I want to leave now.
The crabs have taken my children (my dog, my beach chair).
When will the rain stop?
Is the kelp jerky fresh?
When will the roads reopen?
This is not a vanilla latte.
Why are there tentacles in my chowder?
Will the rescue boat be here soon?
This is not sushi.
I will pay you to stop playing your concertina.
Will there be power today?
Please shoot me.